| 6 JOHN QUINCY ADAMS 1825–29 | 7 ANDREW JACKSON 1829–37 | 8 MARTIN VAN BUREN 1837–41 | 9 WILLIAM HENRY HARRISON 1841 | JOHN TYLER 1841–45 |

16 ABRAHAM LINCOLN 1861–65

17 ANDREW JOHNSON 1865–69

18 ULYSSES S. GRANT 1869–77

19 RUTHERFORD B. HAYES 1877–81

20 JAMES A. GARFIELD 1881

27 WILLIAM HOWARD TAFT 1909–13

28 WOODROW WILSON 1913–21

34 DWIGHT D. EISENHOWER 1953–61

THE WHITE HOUSE HAS BEEN THE HOME AND OFFICE TO EVERY PRESIDENT OF THE UNITED STATES SINCE JOHN ADAMS.

35 JOHN F. KENNEDY 1961–63

41 GEORGE H. W. BUSH 1989–93

42 WILLIAM J. CLINTON 1993–2001

43 GEORGE W. BUSH 2001–09

44 BARACK OBAMA 2009–17

45 DONALD J. TRUMP 2017–

MW00636255

Presidents Play!

Sports and the White House

Illustrated by **John Hutton** • Text by **Jonathan Pliska**

THE WHITE HOUSE *HISTORICAL ASSOCIATION*

Introduction

Kids and adults of all ages—even the President of the United States—
enjoy their favorite sports.

The president works very hard in the White House, but this
big house and its yard provide a special place to take a break
for exercise too. As you will learn from the stories in this
book, President Abraham Lincoln rode horses and President
Harry Truman liked to take long walks. President Gerald Ford liked
to swim and President Bill Clinton ran outside on a track. President
Barack Obama shot hoops on the basketball court and President
Dwight Eisenhower putted golf balls.

Presidents also welcome sports champions to
the White House to celebrate their achievements.

White House history is filled with sports
history. In this book you will find out if there is a
president who shared your favorite sport, game,
or exercise to play or watch.

Stewart D. McLaurin
President, White House Historical Association

Let's visit the White House!

This is Lyndon Johnson in the Oval Office. All the presidents work hard here.

But sometimes they take a break to have fun and exercise, like Ronald Reagan.

President Harry Truman took walks.

President Bill Clinton ran on a special jogging track.

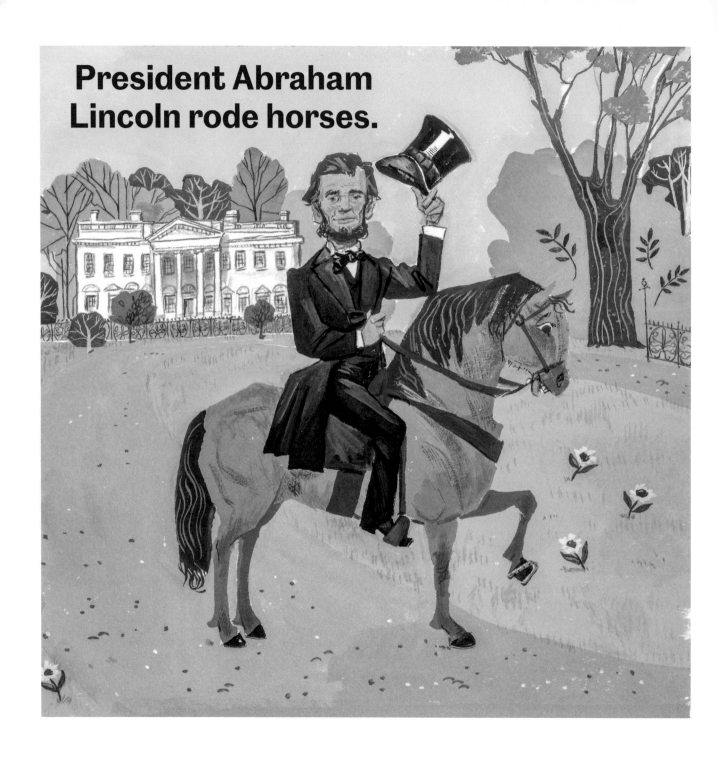

President Abraham
Lincoln rode horses.

Father and son presidents, the George Bushes, pitched horseshoes.

President John Quincy Adams swam in Tiber Creek.

An indoor pool was built for President Franklin D. Roosevelt.

An outdoor pool was built for President Gerald Ford.

President John F. Kennedy enjoyed sailing on the water . . .

. . . while President Grover Cleveland relaxed by fishing.

Back at the White House, President Richard Nixon enjoyed bowling . . .

. . . and President Theodore Roosevelt practiced jujitsu!

But most sports are played outside. President Jimmy Carter liked tennis.

President Barack Obama used the same court for basketball.

And there is a putting green for golf, a favorite of President Dwight D. Eisenhower.

President Herbert Hoover made up a game called Hoover Ball.

Many presidents, like Donald Trump, invite winning teams to the White House.

And others, like President William Taft, throw out the first pitch at baseball games!

When they aren't playing sports, presidents
have fun watching them too, just like you do!

About the Author

Jonathan Pliska is a landscape historian and author of *The White House Easter Egg Roll: A History for All Ages*. He lives in Baltimore County, Maryland.

About the Illustrator

John Hutton is a professor of art history at Salem College, where he has taught since 1990 and is the author of *How to Draw the Presidents*. He lives in Winston-Salem, North Carolina.